BY
JANE SARNOFF
AND
REYNOLD RUFFINS
Consultant
BRUCE PANDOLFINI
U.S. Chess Master

Charles Scribner's Sons
New York

TO BEN, BRADLEY, DAFNA, DANIEL,
DANIELLA, LISE, LYNN, MARK, SETH,
TODD, BORIS AND BOBBY.

Text Copyright © 1973 Jane Sarnoff. Illustrations Copyright © 1973 Reynold Ruffins.
This book published simultaneously in the United States of America and in Canada—Copyright under the Berne Convention. All rights reserved.
No part of this book may be reproduced in any form without the permission of Charles Scribner's Sons.

3 5 7 9 11 13 15 17 19 RD/C 20 18 16 14 12 10 8 6 4 2

Printed in the United States of America. Library of Congress Catalog Card Number 73-1385. SBN 684-13494-2 (cloth)

Chess is an exciting game — full of surprises. It is a game which is always played by the same rules, but it is seldom played the same way twice.

In chess you have to watch your own moves carefully — and the other player's moves even more carefully. At least two things are always happening at the same time in a chess game. When you see only one thing happening, look again. And again.

The objective of a chess game is to capture the opposing King. But the purpose of playing chess is to enjoy yourself. **The Chess Book** will help you to do that. Keep a chessboard and chessmen in front of you as you read and follow the diagrams in the book with them.

Certainly, no book will turn you into a master player, but **The Chess Book** may start you on your way.

There is an Indian proverb that says:
Chess is a sea in which a gnat may drink
and an elephant may bathe.

the Chessmen

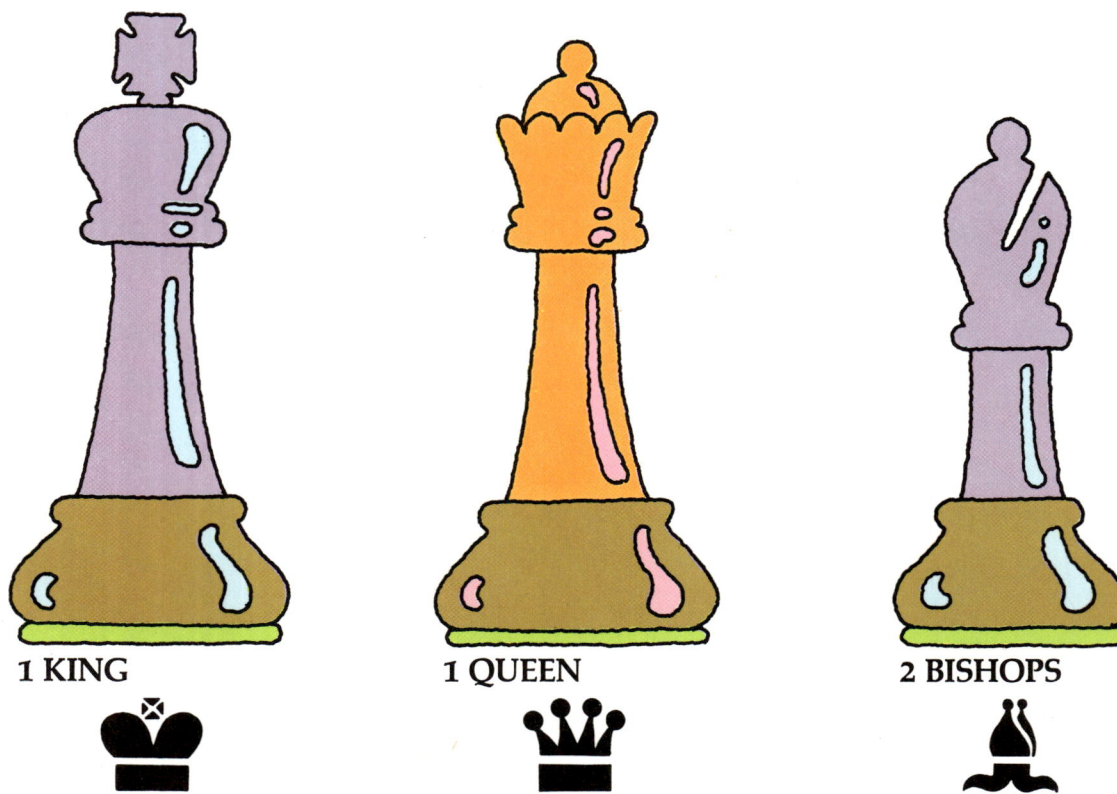

Each player starts the game with 16 chessmen.

The chessmen—and the player—on one side of the board are called White. The chessmen and the player on the other side of the board are called Black. Even if the chessmen are pink and purple, the lighter set is always White, the darker set is always Black.

The term chess "piece" means all the men except Pawns. Kings, Queens, Rooks, Knights and Bishops are chess pieces; Pawns are Pawns. The right term to use when talking about pieces and Pawns is chess**men**—even though one of the pieces is a Queen.

Howard Staunton designed what we now think of as standard chessmen in 1849. His chessmen, and the symbols for them, are used in almost every tournament and in most books

2 KNIGHTS

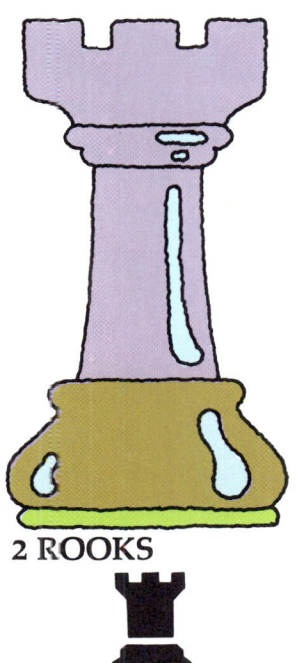

2 ROOKS

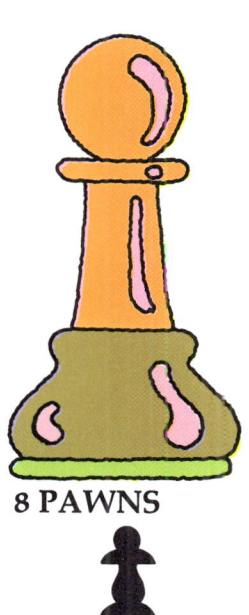

8 PAWNS

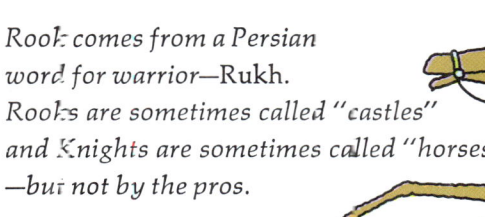

Rook comes from a Persian word for warrior—Rukh. Rooks are sometimes called "castles" and Knights are sometimes called "horses" —but not by the pros.

the Chessboard

The chessboard is made up of 64 squares—32 white squares and 32 black squares. And again, no matter what the **real** colors of the squares are, the lighter is always White and the darker is always Black.

The squares are arranged in 8 rows of 8 squares each, with white squares and black squares alternating.

The board is always placed so that the right-hand corner nearest each player is a white square.

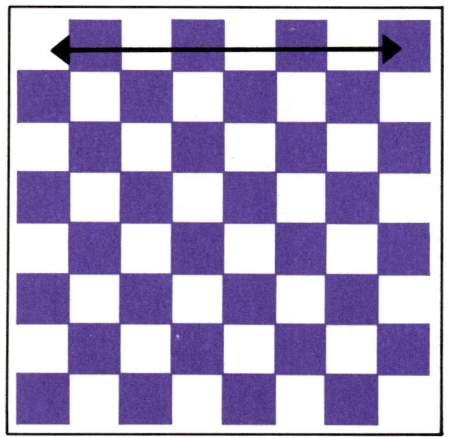

Chessmen may move on the rank (any straight line of squares across the board) or;

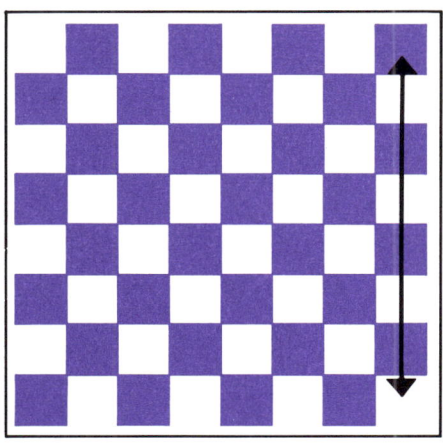

chessmen may move on the file (any straight line of squares up and down the board) or;

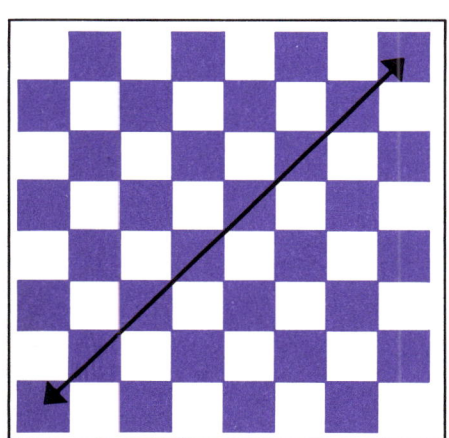

chessmen may move on the diagonal (any straight line of squares that meet at one corner only).

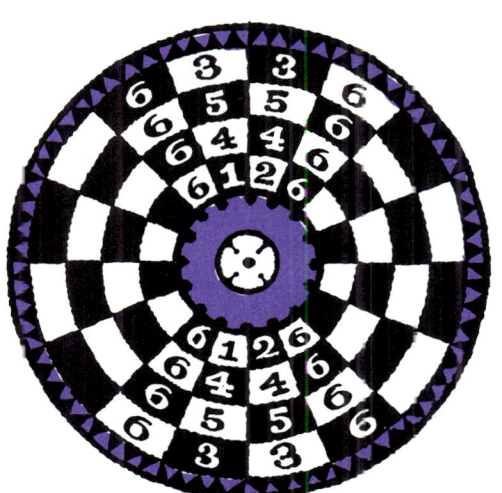

In the Middle Ages, a round chessboard was experimented with. The numbers show the places of the chessmen:
1 King, 2 Queen, 3 Rook, 4 Knight, 5 Bishop, 6 Pawn.

putting the chessmen on the chessboard

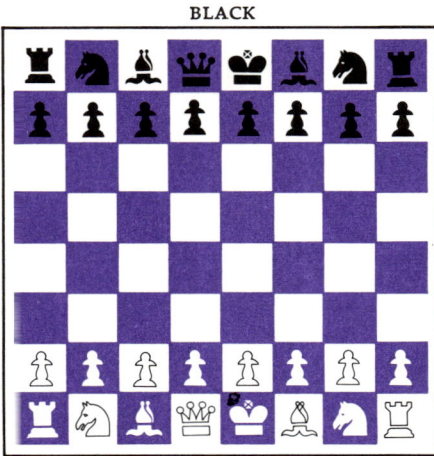

1. All of White's chess **pieces** go on White's 1st rank. All of Black's chess pieces go on Black's 1st rank. The 1st rank for each player is the line of squares closest to each player. Remember where the white corner squares go.

2. The Rooks go in the corners—one on a white square, one on a black.

5. The Queen goes on the remaining square that is the same color as the piece. The rule is **Queen on color**. The White Queen goes on a white square; the Black Queen goes on a black square.

6. The King goes on the last open square in the 1st rank. The White King goes on a black square; the Black King goes on a white square.

3. The Knights go on the next squares in —one on a white square, one on a black.

4. The Bishops go on the next squares in —one on a white square, one on a black.

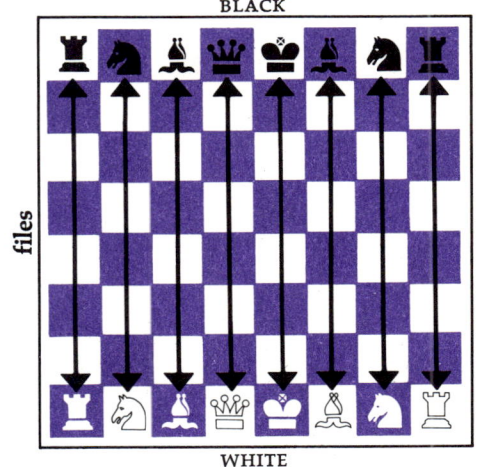

7. The chess pieces should be facing each other at opposite ends of the files. The Black Rooks face the White Rooks. The Black Knights face the White Knights. The Black Bishops face the White Bishops. The Black Queen faces the White Queen. The Black King faces the White King.

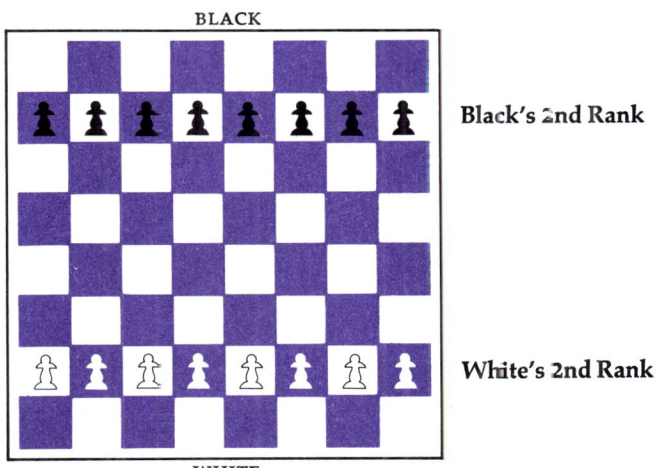

8. The Pawns are put, one to a square, on each player's 2nd rank.

"No, sir, it's not a code. They're playing chess."

how chessmen move and capture

general rules

1. White and Black take turns in moving, but White always moves first.

2. No turn can be skipped, even if the only possible move puts the player in danger.

3. Only one chessman can be moved in a turn. (Except in castling, see page 24.)

4. A move is completed when one chessman has been moved from one square to another. If a chessman is touched, it must be moved, even into danger or capture.

5. Only one chessman can occupy a square at a time.

6. No chessman, except the Knight, can leap over a square that is occupied by another chessman of either side. (Except in castling, see page 24.)

7. Each chessman, except the Knight, must move in only one direction in a turn.

8. Only one capture can be made in a turn, but no capture has to be made unless it is the only move that will save the King from capture.

9. A player doesn't have to make any particular move unless it is the only move that will save the King from capture.

10. No move or capture can be made that will allow the King to be captured.

In the sixteenth century, the Great Akbar of India built a giant chessboard on his palace grounds. He used real horses, elephants and camels for pieces, and serving boys and some of his wives as Pawns.

In early Indian warfare, battles were decided by the death or capture of the King. The Indians used the same objective in chessboard battles.

the King

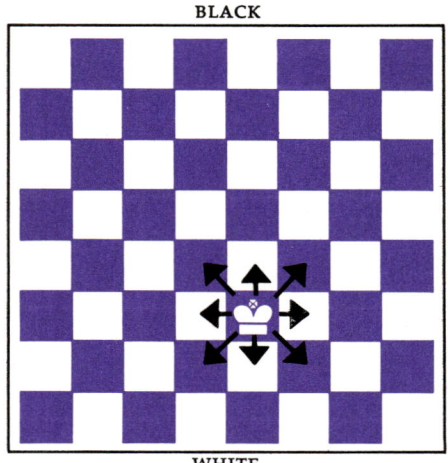

The King moves 1 square at a time on a rank, file, or diagonal. It can move in any direction—forward, backward, sideways or diagonally.

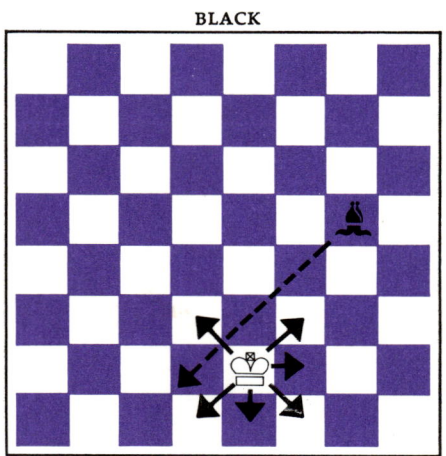

The King cannot move into check. (See page 28.)

The King captures any opposing chessman that is on the square to which the King moves. A captured chessman is removed from the board. The King, and all the other chessmen, can only capture one man at a time.

the Queen

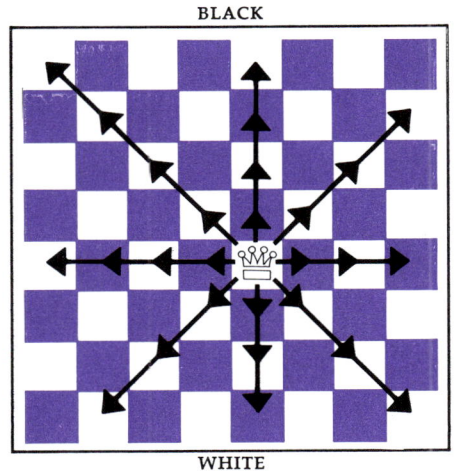

The Queen may move from 1 to 7 squares at a time.

The Queen moves in a straight line on a rank, file, or diagonal. It can move forward, backward, sideways or diagonally, as long as none of the squares in its path is occupied. (No chessman, except the Knight, can jump over its own or opposing chessmen.)

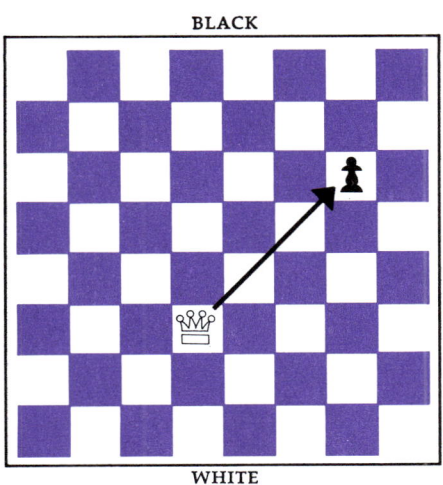

The Queen captures any opposing chessman that is on the square to which the Queen moves.

the Rook

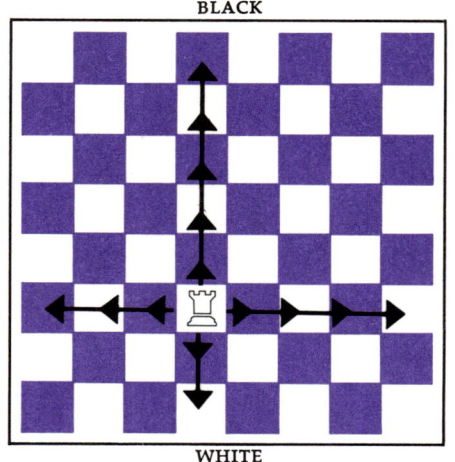

The Rook may move from 1 to 7 squares at a time.

The Rook moves in a straight line on rank or file. It can move backward, forward, or sideways as long as none of the squares in its path is occupied.

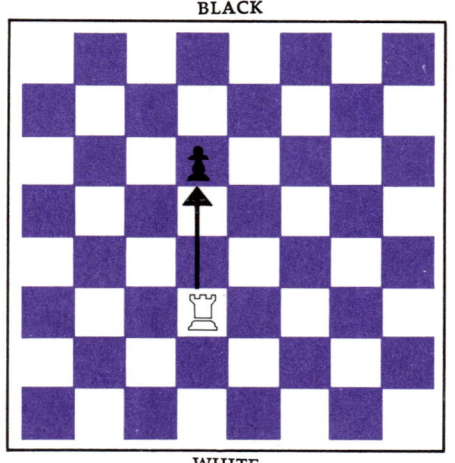

The Rook captures any opposing chessman that is on the square to which the Rook moves.

the Knight

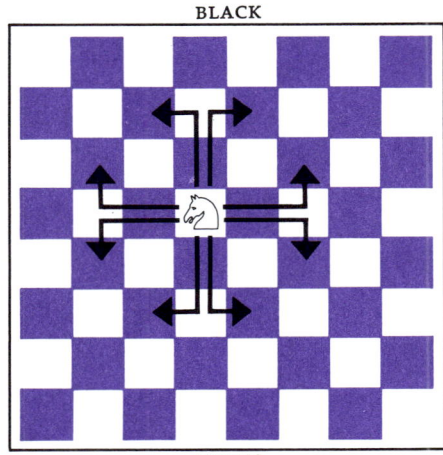

The Knight **always** moves 3 squares at a time.

The Knight moves in an 'L' shaped pattern on the rank and file. The Knight first moves 2 squares in a straight line (sideways, backward or forward) and then one square to the left or right.

The Knight will always land on a square that is the opposite color of the one from which the move started.

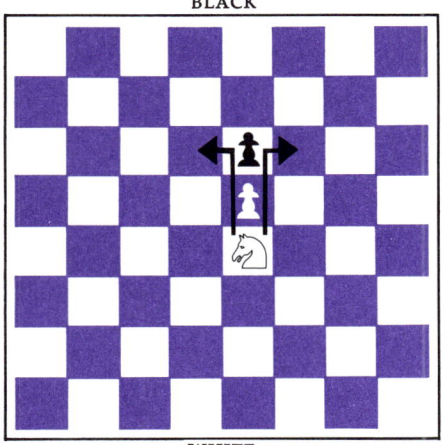

The Knight is the only piece that **can** jump over its own or opposing chessmen.

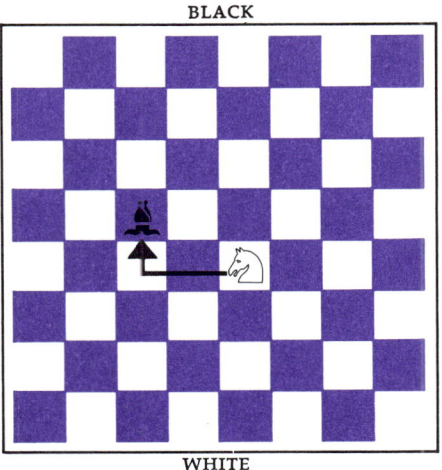

The Knight captures any opposing chessman that is on the square to which the Knight moves.

the Bishop

The Bishop may move from 1 to 7 squares at a time.

The Bishop moves only on the diagonal, on squares that are the same color as the square on which the Bishop was placed at the beginning of the game. The Bishop that started the game on the black square must stay on the black squares. The Bishop that started on the white square must stay on the white squares.

The Bishop moves in either direction on a diagonal, as long as none of the squares in its path is occupied.

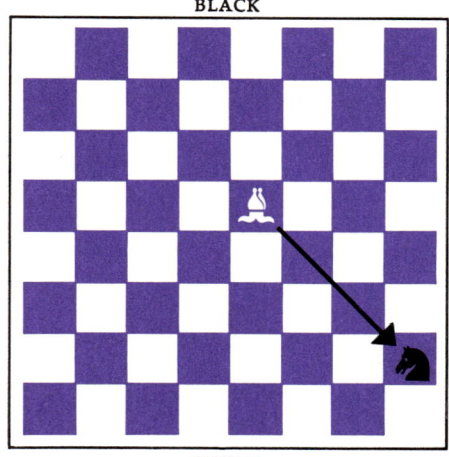

The Bishop captures any opposing chessman that is on the square to which the Bishop moves.

the Pawn

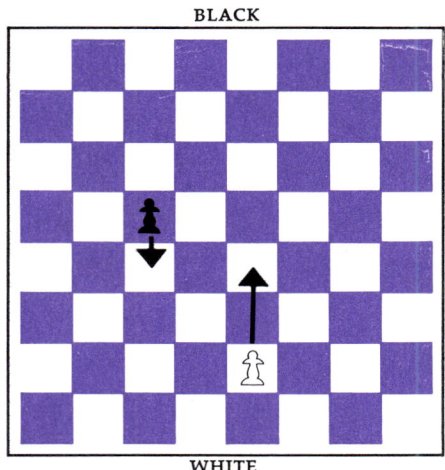

The Pawn can only move in one direction—forward. It moves on its own file, 1 square at a time.

On each Pawn's first move **only**, it can choose to move forward 2 squares. The Pawn cannot capture on a 2-square move. (See *en passant* capture, page 26.)

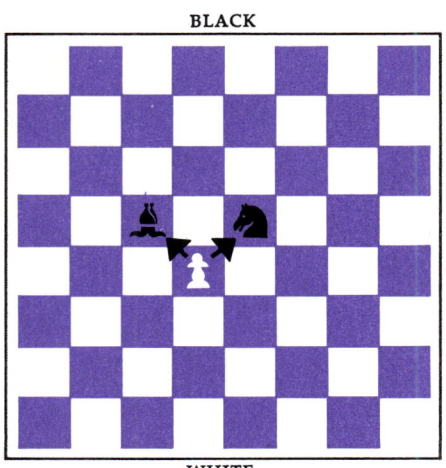

The Pawn is the only chessman that captures in a way different from the way it moves. The Pawn captures by taking the chessman that occupies either square diagonally ahead of it. The Pawn then occupies the square that the captured man was on. The next time the Pawn moves, it goes straight ahead on the file it is on. The Pawn **moves** straight ahead, but it **captures** diagonally ahead.

The Pawn cannot move when a chessman is directly in front of it. Even if the Pawn is blocked from **moving** straight ahead, it can still capture diagonally.

more about moving and capturing

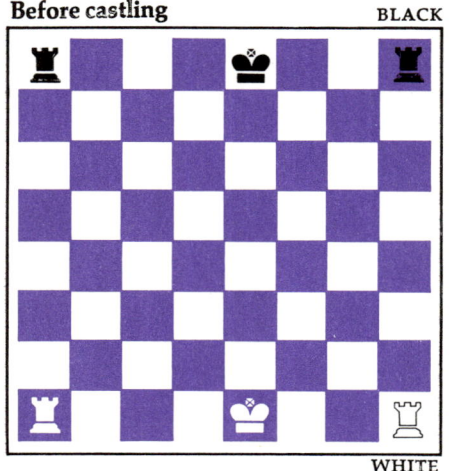
Before castling

castling

Castling is the only time in the game when two pieces are moved at the same time: the King and one of the Rooks. The move gets the King away from the exposed center file and over to a side file where it is harder for the opposing forces to get to it. Pawns are often left in front of a castled King for extra protection. Castling also gets the Rook away from the corner file and into a center file where it can be better used to attack the opposing force. **Castle early in the game.**

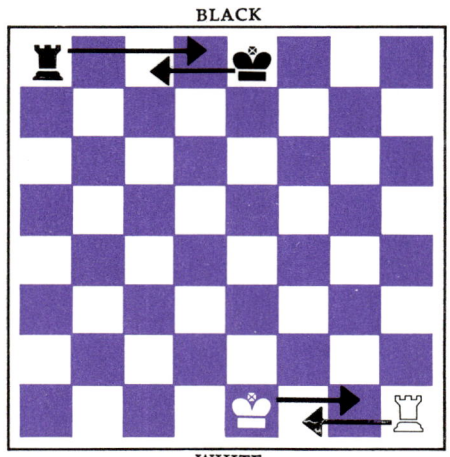

To castle, the King moves 2 squares toward a Rook and then the Rook moves to the square that the King **passed over**. The King must be moved first. If the Rook is touched first, only the Rook can be moved.

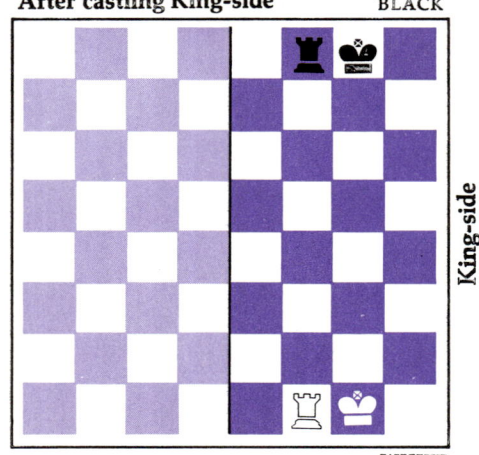
After castling King-side

The King can castle on the King-side, with the King and the King-Rook. (See page 32.)

The King can castle on the Queen-side, with the King and the Queen-Rook. (See page 32.)

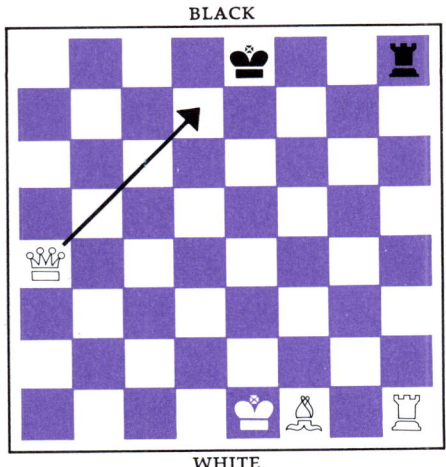

The King cannot castle if the King is in check. (See page 28 for check.)

The King cannot castle if there is a chessman between the King and the Rook.

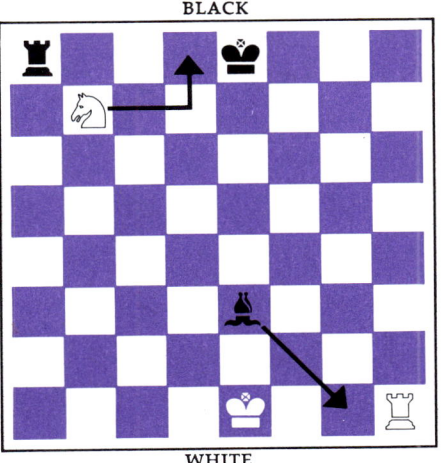

The King cannot castle if the square the King has to pass over is under attack.

The King **can** castle if the Rook must pass over a square that is under attack.

The King cannot castle if the square the King wishes to move to is under attack.

Note: Each player can castle only once during a game.

Pawn en passant capture

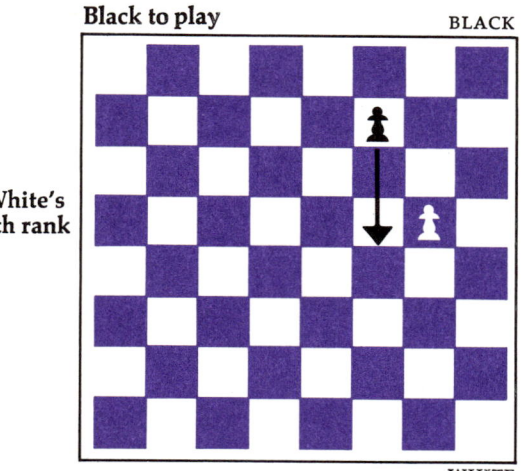

When a Pawn advances to its own 5th rank, it can capture an opposing Pawn in a special way called *en passant* (in passing).

If an opposing Pawn moves 2 squares on its first move, the 5th-rank Pawn may capture it **as if it had moved only one square.**

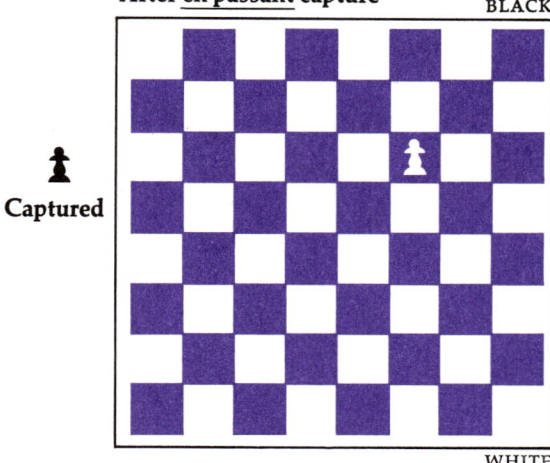

When an *en passant* capture is made, the capturing Pawn removes the captured Pawn from the board and goes to the square where the captured Pawn **would have been if it had moved only 1 square**.

The Pawn wanting to make an *en passant* capture must do so on the next move after the opposing Pawn has moved its 2 squares, or not do it at all.

Pawn promotion

Black's 1st rank
White's 8th rank

If a Pawn gets all the way to the opposing side's 1st rank (the Pawn's 8th rank), the Pawn must be promoted to Queen, Rook, Knight or Bishop. The player may choose the kind of piece to which the Pawn is promoted. The Pawn will then move as if it were the piece it has been promoted to.

Pawns can be promoted even though the original Queen, Rooks, Knights and Bishops are still on the board. If all of White's Pawns were promoted to Queen, there would be 9 White Queens. Or, White could have instead, 10 Rooks or 10 Bishops or 10 Knights, or a combination of pieces.

Most of the time the Pawn is promoted to Queen since the Queen is the strongest piece on the board.

Don't underrate Pawns! At the end of the game, if one player has no Pawns and the other has one, that Pawn can get promoted and win the game.

The word Pawn comes from a Spanish word peón which means worker. In fifteenth-century England, Pawns were carved to look like different workers. The Rook-Pawns were farm workers, the Knight-Pawns were iron workers, the Bishop-Pawns were innkeepers, the King-Pawns were bankers and the Queen-Pawns were doctors. It was not until the eighteenth century that all the Pawns were made to look alike.

check

Black to play
BLACK

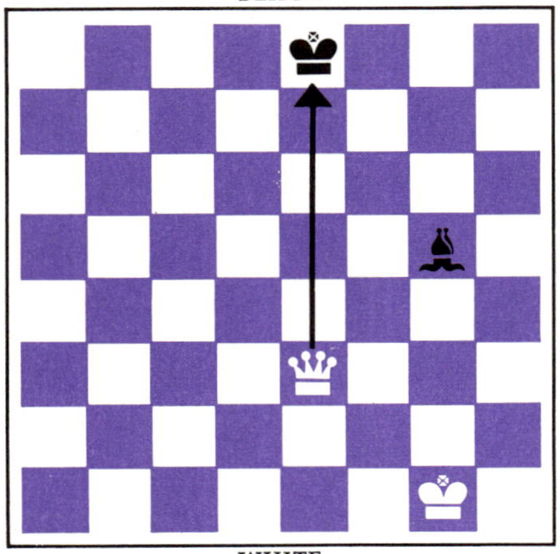

WHITE

The White Queen is checking the Black King.

A King is in check if it can be captured. The attacking player warns the opposing player that the King is in a position to be captured by saying "check." The player whose King is under attack must find a way to get out of check.

Black to play
BLACK

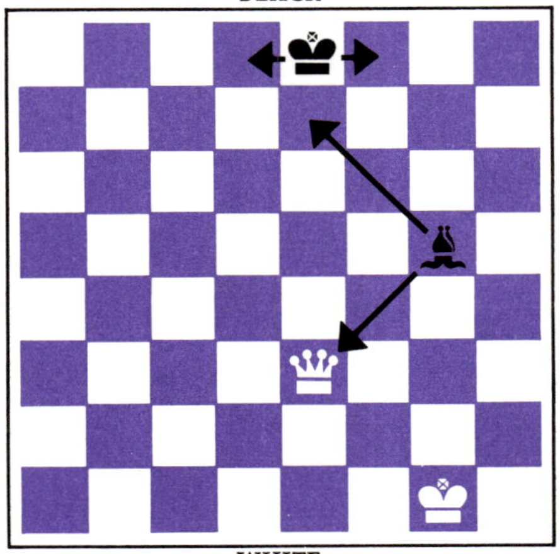

WHITE

Black can move the Bishop into the line of attack, use the Bishop to capture the White Queen, or move the King. Capturing the Queen would be best.

A King can be gotten out of check by: moving another chessman into the line of attack, or capturing the attacking chessman, or moving the King.

checkmate and stalemate

Black to play—and can't

The Black King is checkmated. Any moves the Black King could make would put it in check by the White King or Queen. "Mate" and game to White.

If the King cannot get out of check, the King is checkmated, or mated. The attacking player announces "mate" and the game is over.

Black to play—stalemate

Black is **not** in check, but the only moves the Black King could make would put it in check—and the King is not **allowed** to put itself in check. Black is stalemated, but the game is a draw.

A player is stalemated if there are no legal moves that can be made. When a player is stalemated, the King is **not** in check, but the only moves that can be made, by the King or any other man, would put the King in check. The player who is stalemated **does not lose the game**. The game is a draw. It may seem unfair—but that's the rule.

One day in Denmark in the twelfth century, King Knud V was playing chess with another King, Valdemar. An enemy, King Sweyn, sneaked into the room where the two were playing and killed King Knud. King Valdemar escaped by using his chessboard as a shield.

The word checkmate comes from two Persian words: Sháh, **which means King, and** mát, **which means helpless.**

everything in chess has an exact name

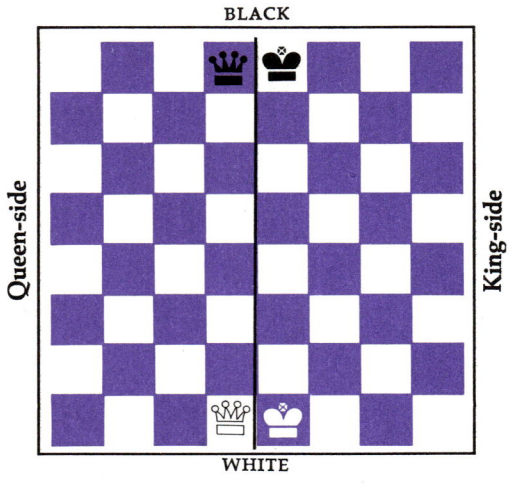

The half of the board the Queens are on is called the Queen-side. The half the Kings are on is the King-side.

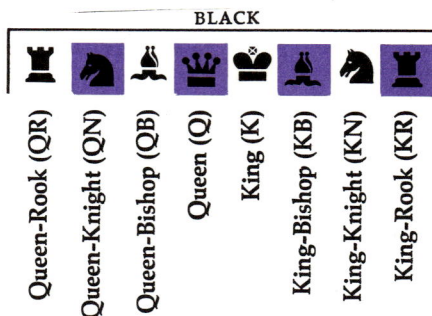

The pieces on the Queen-side are called the Queen-Rook, Queen-Knight, Queen-Bishop.

The pieces on the King-side are called King-Rook, King-Knight, King-Bishop. The Kings and Queens are called just that.

Often the names of the pieces are abbreviated to their first letters. In this book, 'N' is used as the abbreviation for Knight to avoid a mix-up with the 'K' abbreviation for King. In some books Knight is abbreviated 'Kt.'.

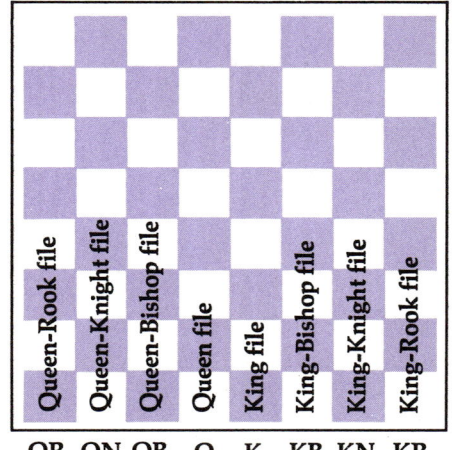

Each file is named for the piece that stands on it at the beginning of the game.

At the beginning of the game, the Pawns are named for the files on which they stand: Queen-Rook-Pawn, Queen-Knight-Pawn, Queen-Bishop-Pawn, Queen-Pawn, King-Pawn, King-Bishop-Pawn, King-Knight-Pawn, King-Rook-Pawn. As the game goes on, all Pawns are abbreviated 'P'. When it is necessary, to avoid a mix-up, to explain exactly **which** Pawn is moving or being captured, the Pawn is given the name of the file it is on at the time.

Each rank has two numbers. The rank closest to White is White's 1st rank and also Black's 8th rank. The rank closest to Black is Black's 1st rank and also White's 8th rank. And so on.

When the numbers of the ranks and the names of the files are put together, each square on the board has two names—which are almost always abbreviated by letter and number.

The darker square names on the top are Black's names for the squares. The lighter square names on the bottom are White's names for the squares.

When White moves to a square, use the White name for the square. When Black moves to a square, use the Black name for the square.

When it is very clear what is happening on the board, the names and abbreviations for chessmen and squares are shortened even more. Most often, the King- and Queen-part of the name or abbreviation is dropped.

Abbreviations are always used to keep track of the moves in a game. On the first move of a game, for example: "The Pawn in front of the King moves to the 4th rank of the King file" is abbreviated P—K4.

P—K4 is the most common move to start a game. And so, on with the game. . . .

Ways to write chess moves

- — moves to
- x captures
- o-o castles King-side
- o-o-o castles Queen-side
- e.p. en passant
- ch check
- ! good move
- !! very good move
- ? bad move
- ?? very bad move
- !? may be good or bad but probably good move
- ?! may be good or bad but probably bad move

33

sample game

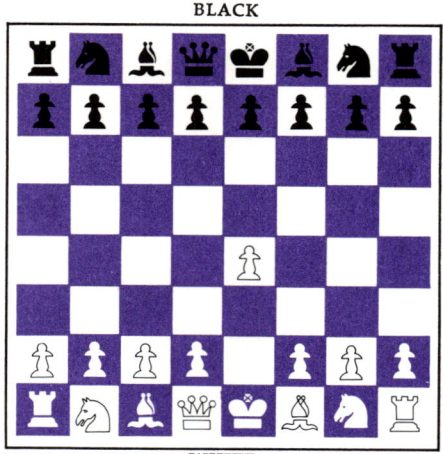

Scholar's Mate
The entire game reads:

White (you)	**Black** (your opponent)
1 P—K4	P—K4
2 B—B4	B—B4
3 Q—R5	N—QB3??
4 QxBP mate	

White's first move is P—K4. (The Pawn in front of the King has moved 2 squares to White's 4th rank.) Remember White **always** moves first.

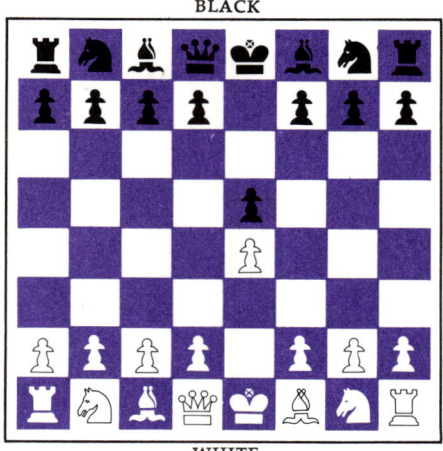

Black replies with the same move: P—K4. This move, for either side, opens up the diagonal that the King-Bishop moves on and allows the King-Bishop to get into the game.

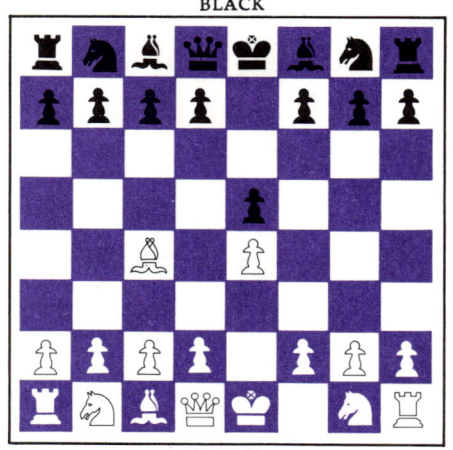

White then moves the King-Bishop to the 4th rank of the Queen-Bishop file (B—B4). It is a good idea to get the King-Bishop and the King-Knight out onto the field as soon as possible so that you can castle early.

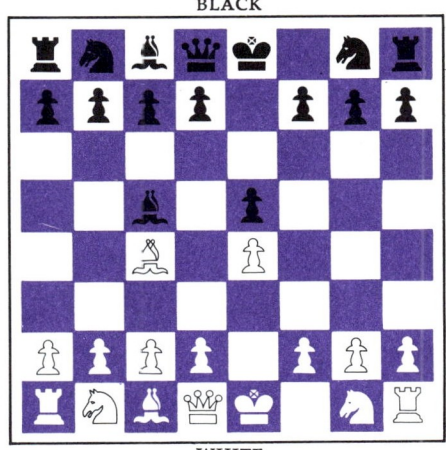

Black replies by moving the King-Bishop to the 4th rank of the Queen-Bishop file (B—B4). Of course, the Bishops cannot capture each other because Bishops move and capture on the diagonal.

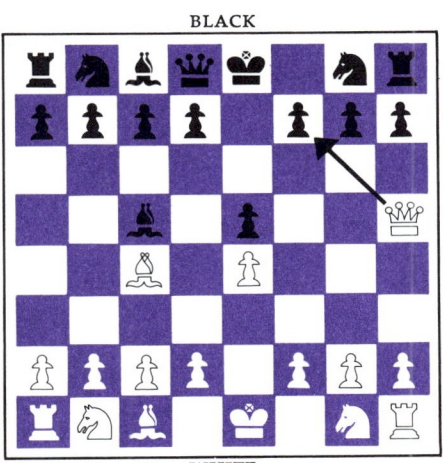

White's next move is Q—R5. (The Queen is moved to the 5th rank in the King-Rook file.)

With this move, White's Queen threatens to capture Black's Bishop-Pawn—checkmating Black. (QxBP checkmate.)

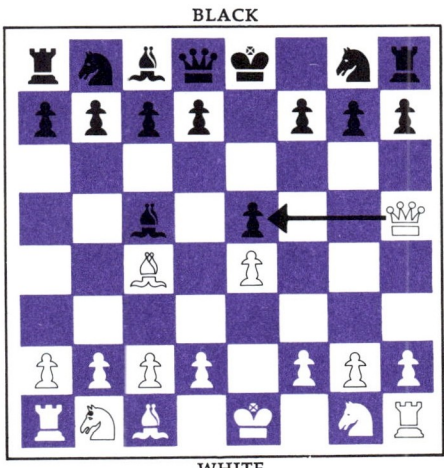

With the same move (Q—R5), White's Queen threatens to capture the Black King-Pawn. If the King-Pawn is captured, the White Queen can put the Black King in check. If White made that move it would be written QxKP ch. Notice carefully the difference here between check and checkmate.

Scholar's Mate was first recorded in England in 1640.

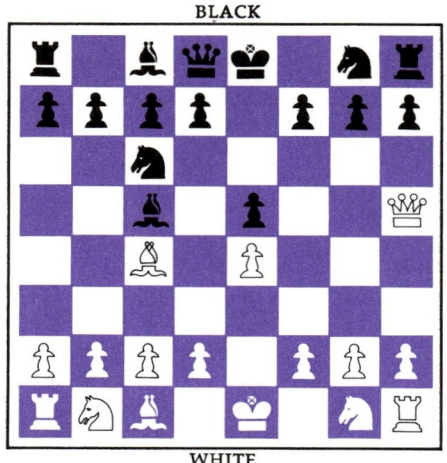

Black notices the second threat to the King-Pawn, but does not notice the first threat to the Bishop-Pawn. Black, therefore, makes a very bad move (??) N—QB3. Black hopes to capture the White Queen with the Knight if the Queen captures Black's King-Pawn.

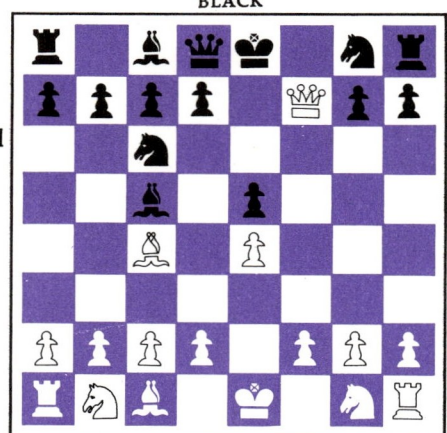

White moves the Queen to the 7th rank in the King-Bishop file and captures Black's Bishop-Pawn (QxBP checkmate). The Black King is checkmated—there is no place the Black King can move, no man to put in the way of the White Queen to defend the Black King, and no man that can capture the White Queen.

The Black King cannot capture the White Queen because the Black King would be putting itself in check with the White Bishop—and that's not a legal move.

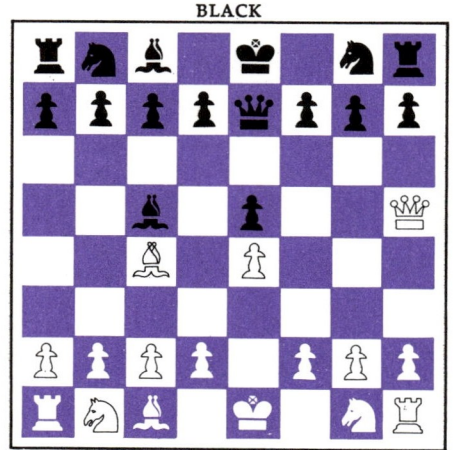

What Black could have done on the 3rd move was Q—K2. That move would have guarded the Black King-Pawn **and** protected the Black King from the threatened checkmate.

With your board and men, play out these moves which Black could have made for a 3rd move and see what happens:
3 . . . Q—B3, 3 . . . P—KN3, 3 . . . N—KR3.
Since White always moves first, if you want to show Black's move without White's, it is written with the number of the move followed by (. . .).

starting strategy

Note: Set up your chessmen and board and play out the strategy as you read.

The four squares in the center of the board are very important—they get most of the action. You should try to control these squares by having men aimed at them or having men in a position where they can attack an opposing chessman on one of the squares.

The need to control the four center squares is one reason why a good first move is to move the King-Pawn 2 squares. The move puts your Pawn on one of the center squares and opens up diagonal pathways for the Queen and the King-Bishop. By using those pathways, the Queen and the King-Bishop are aimed at the center squares.

Another good first move is to move the Queen-Pawn 2 squares into a center square. What pathways will that move open up?

Moving the King-Knight or the King-Bishop next is a good plan. It will help you to castle early in the game and get the Rook into play.

When you move the Knight out, remember that the Knight's second move should be aimed at one of the four center squares—not off to one side out of the action.

Unless a chessman is under attack, don't keep moving it around—especially if it controls or threatens any of the four center squares. Instead, bring out one of your other chessmen and start moving your entire force toward the opposing King.

Do not move any of your men into a line of attack unless you have a good reason for sacrificing one.

A **bad** opening would be to move the Rook-Pawns. Moving them won't help you control the center of the board and won't open a pathway for the Rooks. It won't open a pathway for the Knights either since the Knights can leap over their own men.

VALUE OF CHESSMEN

Queen — 9 points
Rook — 5 points
Knight — 3 points
Bishop — 3 points
Pawn — 1 point

Knowing the value of the men will help you decide when to capture an opposing chessman if the capture means sacrificing a man of your own.

There are 169,518,829,100,544,000,000,000,000 possible ways to play the first 10 moves in a game of chess.

Ivan the Terrible, the first czar of Russia, died in 1584 while working out a chess problem.

In 9¾ hours on December 13, 1960, Georges Koltanowsky played chess with 56 opponents, one after another, while he was blindfolded. He won 50 games, drew 6 and lost none.

THE EIGHT QUEENS PROBLEM (*A problem for one player*)

Take all the men off the board. Pretend that 8 Pawns of either color are Queens. Set them up on the board in such a way that no Queen is in a position to capture any other Queen. There are 92 ways to solve the problem.

THE KNIGHT'S TOUR
(A problem for one player)

Take all the chessmen off the board except one Knight. The Knight may start anywhere, but must move in its regular way. The Knight must be moved to land <u>just once</u> on every square on the board. There are a number of different ways to solve the problem. To keep track of the moves, draw a chessboard on a piece of paper and mark down the order in which your Knight lands on the squares. The Knight's Tour is a very old chess problem. The answer which is given here (upside down) was first worked out in India in the fourteenth century.

12	15	8	19	44	47	40	35
9	62	11	14	41	36	43	46
16	13	60	7	48	45	34	39
63	10	17	22	37	42	55	50
18	23	6	59	54	49	38	33
3	64	21	26	31	28	51	56
24	19	2	5	58	53	32	29
1	4	25	20	27	30	57	52

One menu in the fifteenth century included a chessboard cake with icing made of brown or white almond milk. The chessmen were made of molded sugar.

LOSING CHESS

In losing chess the winner is the player who can lose all the pieces first, including the King. There is no check and the King can be captured the same way any other piece can. Each side must capture whenever possible. A Pawn can be promoted and exchanged for a King as well as for any other piece. All the other regular chess rules stay the same.

About 200 years ago a machine was built which played chess with all challengers throughout Europe. The mechanical 'Turk' player almost always won. Everyone was very excited about the amazing machine—and got even more excited when a real chess master was found hidden inside.

There is an old English proverb that says:
You may knock your opponent down with a chessboard,
but that does not prove you are the stronger player.